NURTURING WOMEN'S EQUALITY

An Evaluation Tool

Published By CBE International

Copyright CBE International ©2020

CBE International, USA
122 W Franklin Ave, Suite 218, Minneapolis, MN 55404
www.cbeinternational.org
cbe@cbeinternational.org

All rights reserved.
No part of this publication may be reproduced in any form without written permisiion from CBE International.

Cover design: Margaret Lawrence

ISBN: 978-1-939971-97-5 (Print)
ISBN: 978-1-939971-98-2 (PDF)

TABLE OF CONTENTS

Introduction 7

Organizational Structure 10

History and Healing 12

Preaching and Teaching 15

Church Leadership 17

Access and Input 20

Human Resources 23

Culture of Work and Family 26

Resources and Teaching Materials 28

Liturgy and Church Traditions 30

Ministry Activites 32

Recommended Resources 34

INTRODUCTION

Forty-five percent of adults are unchurched in the US. Historically, the majority of those who are unchurched have been men. Today, that gender gap has decreased. According to Barna Group, the "gap has narrowed from 20 points to just 8 points in the last ten years." Additionally, they found that the majority (85%) of American unchurched women are actually de-churched, meaning that they once regularly attended and participated in the life of a local church. The top two reasons given by women for not attending church—competing priorities and busyness— will come as no surprise. What may be surprising is the third reason women reported as contributing to their disengagement from the church—a lack of emotional engagement and support. Nearly half of women respondents (43%) "said they do not feel *any* emotional support *at all* from church" (emphasis added). When almost half the women who are still in church say they feel no emotional support from church, something is deeply wrong.

Research shows that when communities esteem both males and females and invest in their potential equally, these communities are more likely to enjoy flourishing.[1] Both secular and Christian humanitraians increasingly acknowledge the influence of faith leaders in promoting the dignity and agency of females.[2] Recognizing that pastors and lay leaders need to be supported and equipped as they work to create a culture that promotes the flourishing of women as equals, CBE has developed this resource to help churches and organizations evaluate the landscape of their church identity and take steps to identify practices which may be inhibiting their church from being a reflection of God's vision for men and women serving and leading together and thus help them advance the gospel.

This tool was designed to be engaged over a period of weeks or months, though you may choose to undertake the project over a long weekend. Please note that the History and Healing section may take longer if there are significant issues to address. We recommend asking each evaluation participant to answer the questions separately before you begin group conversation, to ensure that responses are independent of influence. Additionally, answers may be more honest if participation is anonymous (except for noting the sex in order to observe patterns). Leaders at all levels should answer these questions, but women and men in the congregation who are not in leadership should also be invited to answer the questions as they pertain to their experience in the church. Compare the different answers. Are men's answers different than women's? Is leadership's perception true to the stated experience of congregants?

This tool will not offer a quantitative measure of how egalitarian your church is, but instead is intended as a starting point for conversation and an impetus for growth. No church projects a perfect reflection of God's vision for biblical equality for women and men. The process of dismantling systems that support dominance can feel overwhelming at times. However, CBE is here to support you. We have a variety of resources available to help churches dive deeper into the issues covered by the evaluation, including both academic and non-academic articles on theological and practical matters as well as tools to help bolster marriages, address and prevent intimate partner violence, interpret the Bible, engage in the ministry of reconciliation, and more. We also publish a list of egalitarian counselors and spiritual directors to support the healing of individuals.

Working toward women's equality isn't easy, yet we believe God calls us to this work. We are praying God will bring light and life to your community through this process. Please contact us if there are other ways we can support your church as you step forward in this journey.

---

1. Ana Revenga, Sudhir Shelly, "Empowering Women Is Smart Economics," International Monetary Fund, *Finance & Development*, March 2012, Vol. 49, No. 1, https://www.imf.org/external/pubs/ft/fandd/2012/03/pdf/revenga.pdf

2. Mimi Haddad, "Theology and Human Flourishing," *Mutuality* blog, June 15, 2020, https://www.cbeinternational.org/resource/article/mutuality-blog-magazine/theology-and-human-flourishing

Church Organization Chart 1

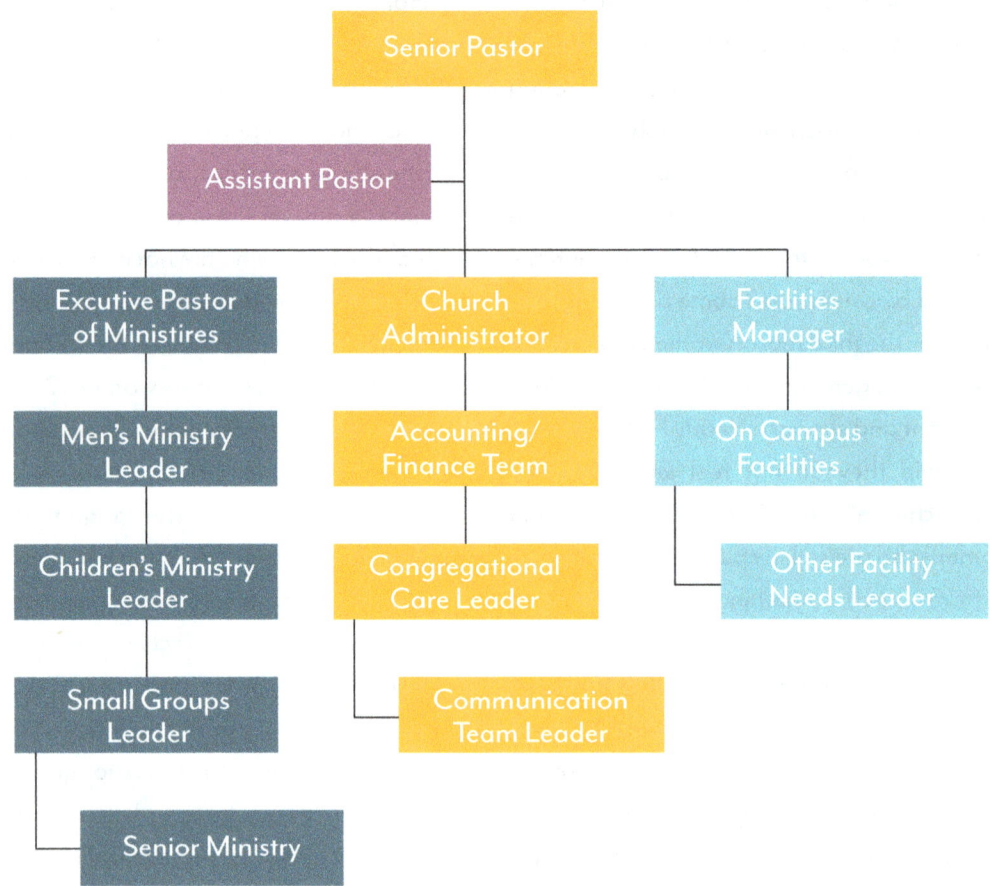

Church Organization Chart 2

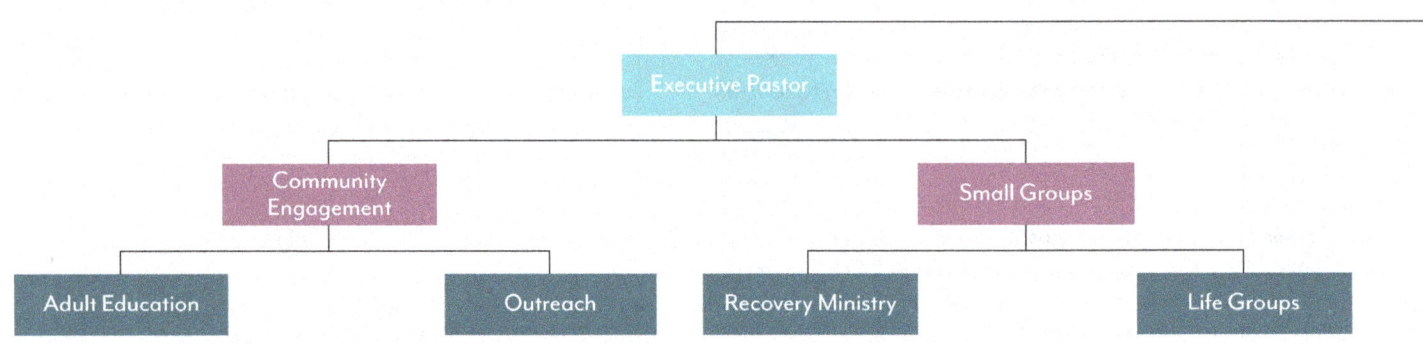

ORGANIZATIONAL MAPPING

Before you begin the evaluation, leaders should map your organization's structure or work from your organizational chart (see examples below).

Account for any hierarchies in leadership and decision-making.

Alongside each role, please note:
- The names of staff or volunteer who fulfill each role.
- Whether the role primarily performs a strategic or operational function. Generally, strategic roles involve directing an organization's movement towards future goals while operational roles are concerned with the day-to-day details and functions of the church.
- Is the position paid or unpaid and what is the amount?

Church Charity Organizational Chart

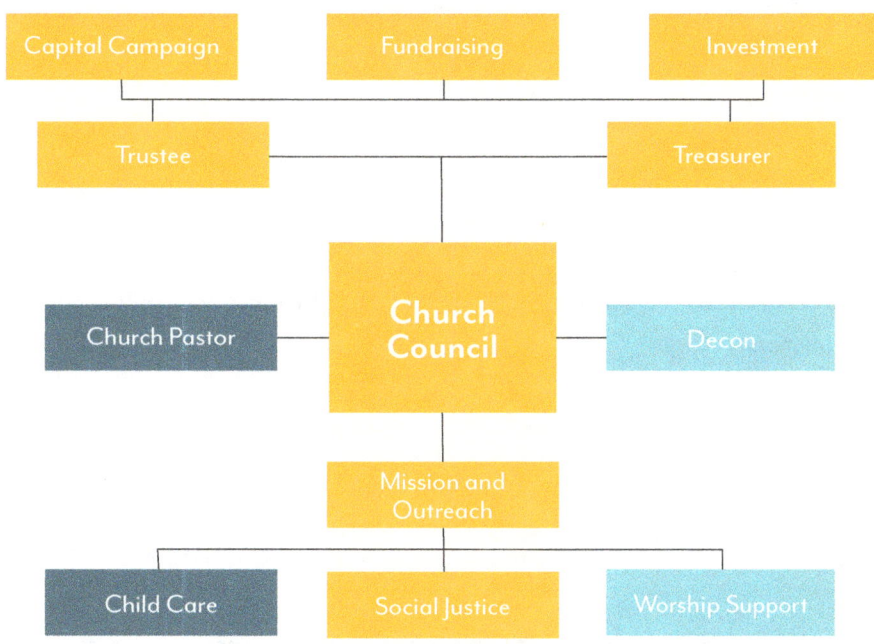

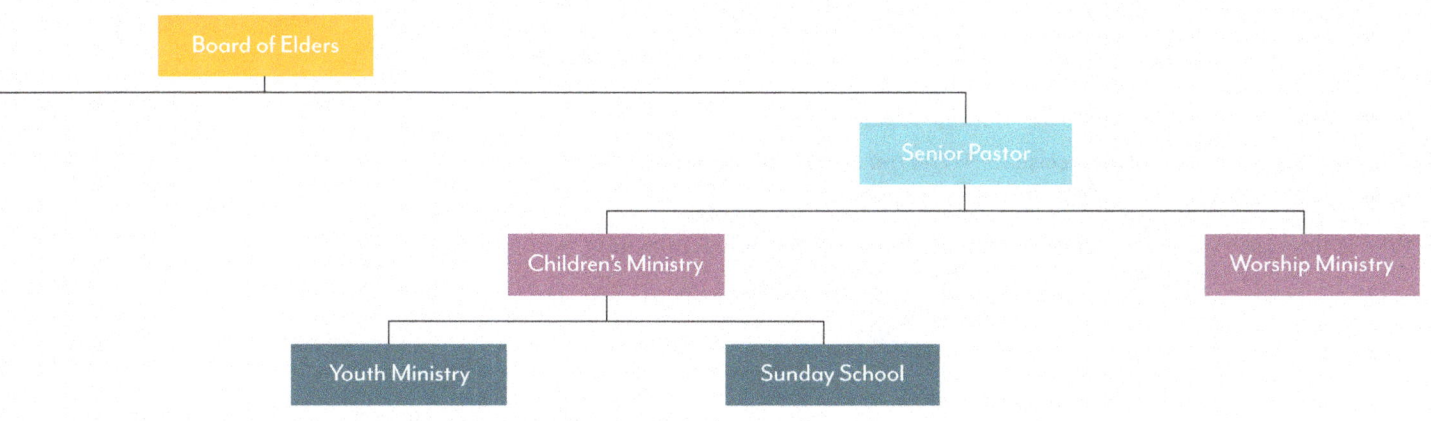

Nurturing Women's Equality - A Church Evaluation Tool

ORGANIZATIONAL STRUCTURE

NOW, TAKE A LOOK AT YOUR ORGINIZATIONAL MAP:
Do strategic roles tend to be filled by men or women? What about the operational roles?

Of all the roles mapped, which roles would you consider most necessary for the functioning of the church? If those roles were not filled, how would the church function?

Is there a difference in the way the church values roles traditionally undertaken by women versus roles traditionally undertaken by men? Note differences in pay, decision-making authority, and both public and interpersonal recognition. What do these differences imply about value and respect for different roles.

Consider:
- Are there any observable patterns in paid vs. unpaid roles?
- Who is sought out for making decisions? Who gets credit for decisions?
- Which positions/roles can make independent decisions?
- Who isgets awarded with attention and recognition by the church body and leaders for performing their role?

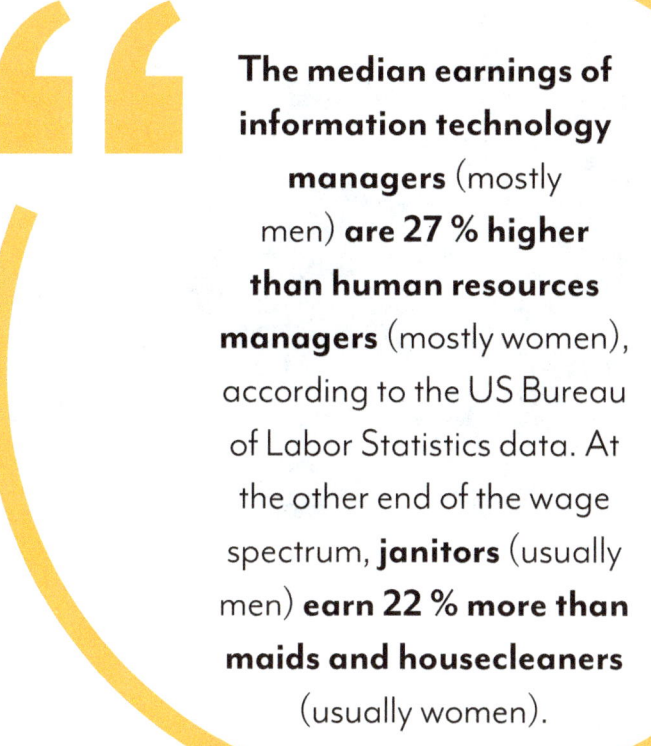

> The median earnings of information technology managers (mostly men) are 27 % higher than human resources managers (mostly women), according to the US Bureau of Labor Statistics data. At the other end of the wage spectrum, janitors (usually men) earn 22 % more than maids and housecleaners (usually women).

READ

As a group, look at 1 Corinthians 1:12–27 and explore the implications for your church and this discussion. Does your church reflect the picture painted by Paul?

EXPLORE

Historically, women were expected to operate within the domain of the home, maintaining the daily operations of family life, including housework, child care, elder care, and food preparation. Men were allowed more freedom to sustain a presence in the public sphere where their voices shaped the strategic direction of institutions like government, science, church, and education. Though both spheres are important, jobs traditionally performed by women are still valued differently, remaining unpaid or underpaid.

Researchers consistently find fields traditionally occupied by women are paid lower than fields traditionally populated by men. Even when jobs require similar education, responsibility, and skills, there remain well-documented gender discrepancies in median earnings. For example, "the median earnings of information technology managers (mostly men) are 27 percent higher than human resources managers (mostly women), according to the US Bureau of Labor Statistics data. At the other end of the wage spectrum, janitors (usually men) earn 22 percent more than maids and housecleaners (usually women)."

Furthermore, once women begin to enter fields traditionally occupied by men, the average pay for that field decreases. The opposite happens, though, when men enter a field previously occupied by women. For example, computer programming "used to be a relatively menial role done by women. But when male programmers began to outnumber females, the job began paying more and gained prestige."

FURTHER READING:

"As Women Take Over a Male-Dominated Field, the Pay Drops." Claire Cain Miller, *The New York Times*, March 19, 2016, https://www.nytimes.com/2016/03/20/upshot/as-women-take-over-a-male-dominated-field-the-pay-drops.html.

"Sticking Women with the Office Housework," Joan C. Williams, *The Washington Post*, April 16, 2014, https://www.washingtonpost.com/news/on-leadership/wp/2014/04/16/sticking-women-with-the-office-housework/.

"The Pay Gap Is Worse for Pastor-Moms," Kate Shellnutt, *Christianity Today*, Augst 3, 2017, https://www.christianitytoday.com/ct/2017/august-web-only/pay-gap-is-worse-for-pastor-moms.html.

HISTORY AND HEALING

READ

"Christian Complicity in the Suffering of Girls and Women," Mimi Haddad, *The Forum on Women, Religion, Violence, and Power at The Carter Center*, May 27, 2015, http://forum.cartercenter.org/sites/default/files/2019-09/Christian%20Complicity.pdf.

REFLECT

What wounds have been inflicted by patriarchy in the historical church? In *your* church?

Are there stories or examples from women in your church or organization who felt belittled, stymied, or held back from being what or who God made them to be?

Are there stories or examples of women in your church or organization who have been affected by purity culture? Expectations for dress? How has it affected their sense of self and their sense of God?

Have leaders been trained to minister to survivors of abuse/trauma/harassment? Has time been taken to address, discuss, and teach on the impact of patriarchy on women in the church?

If women have expressed feelings of unsafety, how have leaders responded? Are women thought to be over-reacting or overly sensitive? What is your church's procedure for responding to reports of abuse or harassment?

Are small groups, youth retreats, and one on one sesions safe for women and girls? Do you require screening (not just background checks, but also references from previous employers, etc.) for volunteers/leaders? What safety mechanisms are in place to prevent abuse or harassment? If a staff or church member has a known history of abuse or harassment, how are others protected?

Is there a program to address healing or reconciliation of those affected by unhealthy theology in their history/history of the church? If not, when will you take time to consider that? How will you engage women and men in grief/lament, healing, and reconciliation?

EXPLORE

"How American Evangelicalism Has Been Weaponized Against Women," Mimi Haddad, *Mutuality* blog, November 15, 2018, https://www.cbeinternational.org/blogs/how-american-evangelicalism-has-been-weaponized-against-women.

"How to Be an Ally to Women in the Church," Hannah Wilkinson, *Mutuatlity* blog, February 27, 2018, https://www.cbeinternational.org/blogs/how-be-ally-women-church.

"Domestic and Gender-Based Violence: Pastors' Attitudes and Actions," LifeWay Research, 2018, http://lifewayresearch.com/wp-content/uploads/2018/09/Domestic-Violence-Research-Report.pdf , accessed October 12, 2020

In a survey of Protestant pastors, Lifeway Research found that pastors drastically underestimate the number of sexual abuse victims in their congregations; a majority of them guessed in the survey that 10 percent or less might be victims. But in 2016, the Centers for Disease Control and Prevention found that 1 in 4 women (women make up approximately 55 percent of evangelicals) and 1 in 9 men have been sexually abused. There is no evidence suggesting those numbers are lower inside the church.

> "While my church leadership team was working on dividing congregants into small groups, multiple female church leaders expressed concern about having mixed small groups that included men with a known history of abuse toward women. An extended conversation occurred. Male church leaders pushed back, treating the women's concerns as overblown. Finally, one of the male leaders spoke up, agreeing with the women. Only then did the other male leaders concede."
>
> —anonymous congregant

The Centers for Disease Control and Prevention found that **1 in 4 women** and **1 in 9 men** have been **sexually abused**.

FURTHER READING

"Clergy Responses to Domestic Violence." Steven R. Tracy, *Priscilla Papers* vol. 21, no. 2 (2007): 9-17, https://www.cbeinternational.org/resource/article/priscilla-papers-academic-journal/clergy-responses-domestic-violence.

"9 Anti-Abuse Practices Your Church Needs to Adopt." Becky Castle Miller, *Mutuality* blog, August 8, 2017, https://www.cbeinternational.org/resource/article/mutuality-blog-magazine/9-anti-abuse-practices-your-church-needs-adopt.

Domestic Violence: What Every Pastor Needs to Know. Al Miles, Minneapolis: Fortress Press, 2011.

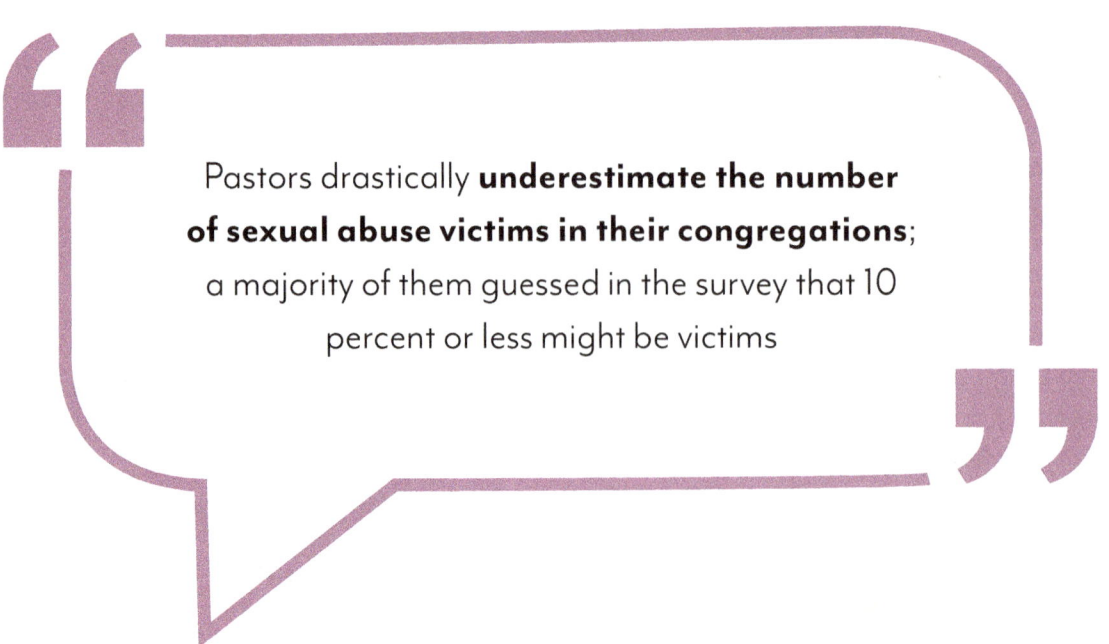

Pastors drastically **underestimate the number of sexual abuse victims in their congregations**; a majority of them guessed in the survey that 10 percent or less might be victims

PREACHING AND TEACHING

READ

"How to Deal with Sexism in Your Church," Jeanne Porter King, *Mutuality* magazine, February 11, 2018, https://www.cbeinternational.org/blogs/how-deal-sexism-your-church.

REFLECT

In sermons, religious education courses, Sunday school classes, and other church teaching, how often is there preaching/teaching about women in the Bible and female leaders in church history?

Are sermons/teachings about those women primarily directed at women? When was the last time a male teacher/preacher taught about a woman in the Bible to a male or mixed audience?

Consider what kind of illustrations/anecdotes/characterizations of women are used in preaching and teaching: What kinds of descriptors are being used about women in the stories? Are the ones used about women demeaning in any way? Are they related to her appearance versus her gifts, calling, and achievements? ("my hot wife" or "beautiful daughters" or "our lovely secretary")?

Have teachers and preachers taken time to examine their assumptions about women and men, and whether they are based on human culture versus God's design?

Which translation of the bible do you most often teach/preach from? Are you aware of its biased language regarding women? Does the translation accurately reflect the original Hebrew and Greek texts? Does it take into account historical or cultural factors?

What answers do you give congregants for tough texts about male headship and female submission, or women speaking in the church? When someone questions The difficult texts, do you feel able to answer with confidence?

EXPLORE

"The View from the Pulpit: Honest Advice for Women," Sally Morgenthaler, et al., *Mutuality* magazine, vol. 16, no. 4 (2009): 4–8, https://www.cbeinternational.org/resource/article/mutuality-blog-magazine/view-pulpit.

"Which Bible to Use?" Alvera Mickelsen, *Priscilla Papers* vol.11, no. 4 (1997): 16-17, https://www.cbeinternational.org/resources/article/priscilla-papers/which-bible-use.

"Five Ways Pastors Unconsciously Reinforce Abuse, and How to Do Better," Natalie Collins, *Mutuality* blog, September 4.2017, https://www.cbeinternational.org/resource/article/mutuality-blog-magazine/five-ways-pastors-unconsciously-reinforce-abuse-and-how-do.

In 2013, the term "smokin' hot wife" was entered into an online Dictionary of Christianese. The entry discussed its seemingly widespread use and debated whether or not it was okay to use in a sermon or public prayer. The author considered the impact on the pastor's wife when the term was used by a pastor, but did not explore the possible impact on other women and men in the congregation.

> *Gender stereotyping and sexist jokes are often used to build rapport, either in personal conversations or during teaching. I recently attended a youth event where the speaker praised his "hot wife" and "beautiful daughters" and told us about the time he evangelized to a woman he described as a stripper. He made sure to let us know that, "I told myself to look at her face, not her chest.*

CHURCH LEADERSHIP

READ

"Womentoring," Bev Murrill, *Mutuality* magazine, vol. 22, no. 1 (2015): 16–20; https://www.cbeinternational.org/resource/article/mutuality-blog-magazine/womentoring.

REFLECT

When you hear the word "leader," what ideas come to mind? Make notes about an ideal leader. Use your imagination to create a picture of how they look, dress, act, communicate, and present themselves.

Describe the personality of a leader. In your opinion, should a leader be aggressive? Cooperative? Do they lead from the front? Do they lead by putting others in the front? Are they loud? Soft-spoken? Assertive? Gentle? How are each of these attributes valued by your community? How are each of these attributes valued by your community? Do they reflect the character of Jesus or other biblical leaders? How are they valued in the men or women who exhibit them today?

Does your image and/or description of leaders reflect traditionally male characteristics? Is it difficult to "picture" or envision a female leader? Elder? Pastor?

Can the women in your church picture themselves as leaders? When asked, do they confidently accept, or do they express doubt? Are women comfortable being assertive in the church? How is a woman received when she is assertive?

How much of your church leadership is female? How have you looked for female leaders? Are you having a hard time recognizing female leaders in your own congregation?

When you consider who has "experience" for a particular leadership role, are you taking into account the different opportunities and/or barriers men and women have encountered within that area and how it might impact what "experience" looks like? What is the difference between being "experienced" and being "qualified?" In interviewing candidates, do you develop questions that test for competence regardless of education or professional positions held? What type of training do you provide for those who are qualified but perhaps not experienced?

What's your church's decision-making process? How does it reflect gendered expectations? Does it test for competence regardless of education or traing? Is it hierarchical? Cooperative? One, central leader versus a team approach? Do leaders explain their thinking before making a decision? Is there a system to ensure each voice is heard, especially under-represented, quieter, or less assertive voices? How are decisions communicated to the church body? Is there time for asking questions? Is there room in the decision-making process for questions or concerns to be addressed/incorporated in the solution?

Do your male leaders have female mentors? Do female leaders have female and male mentors?

At which leadership meetings/activities is childcare available? What implications does this have for women or men who wish to attend these leadership meetings/activities? How easy or hard is it for moms/dads to bring their children with them to minister/volunteer? What assumptions underlie when childcare is or is not provided? (Studies indicate a gendered division of labor persists despite women's entry into the paid labor force, with women continuing to bear the majority of "caring" tasks.)

71% of Protestants, but only **39% of Evangelicals,** were **supportive of female pastors**.

EXPLORE

"Leadership as Service," Mimi Haddad, *Mutuality* blog, October 8, 2008, https://www.cbeinternational.org/blogs/leadership-service.

"Christian Women and Leadership," Roberta Hestenes, *Priscilla Papers* vol. 20, no. 4 (2006): 31–35, https://www.cbeinternational.org/resources/article/priscilla-papers/christian-women-and-leadership.

"Women and Leadership: Public Says Women are Equally Qualified, but Barriers Persist," Kim Parker, Juliana Menasce Horowitz, Molly Rohal, *Pew Research Center,* January 14, 2015, https://assets.pewresearch.org/wp-content/uploads/sites/3/2015/01/2015-01-14_women-and-leadership.pdf.

"The Different Words We Use to Describe Male and Female Leaders," David Smith, et al. , *Harvard Business Review*, May 25, 2018, https://hbr.org/2018/05/the-different-words-we-use-to-describe-male-and-female-leaders.

For starters, in terms of sheer numbers of attributes, we found no gender difference in the number of positive attributes assigned, but women were assigned significantly more negative attributes.

Our research on leadership attributes found significant differences in the assignment of 28 leadership attributes when applied to men and women. While men were more often assigned attributes such as analytical, competent, athletic and dependable, women were more often assigned compassionate, enthusiastic, energetic and organized. Consistent with our results, societal attitudes suggest that women leaders are described as more compassionate (the most assigned attribute overall) and organized than men leaders. In contrast, women were more often evaluated as inept, frivolous, gossip, excitable, scattered, temperamental, panicky, and indecisive, while men were more often evaluated as arrogant and irresponsible.

A huge body of work has found that when women are collaborative and communal, they are not perceived as competent—but when they emphasize their competence, they're seen as cold and unlikable, in a classic "double bind."

"2010 National Survey of Congregations," *Faith Communities Today*, https://faithcommunitiestoday.org/wp-content/uploads/2019/01/2010FrequenciesV1.pdf.

Faith Communities Today 2010 found 12 percent of congregations in the US had a female as senior or sole ordained leader. The numbers are even lower for evangelical congregations, with only 9 percent having a female senior or sole leader. While 71 percent of Protestants are supportive of female pastors, only 39 percent of evangelicals were supportive. Research reported in the book, Women Who Preached the Word, *indicates those numbers are even lower. Despite this, only 12 percent of women felt they'd been treated differently because of their gender and only 3 percent believe they'd been held back because of their gender. These numbers are similar to the expressed sentiment of men (14 percent and 5 percent), except men felt more strongly that they'd been treated differently and held back. Interestingly, according to Pew research, 55 percent of evangelicals are women.*

"Research on Lay Church Members Attitudes toward Women Clergy: An Assessment," *Review of Religious Research*, vol. 28, no. 4. https://www.jstor.org/stable/3511637?seq=1#page_scan_tab_contents.

After contact with women ministers, especially contact in-role, the level of receptivity tends to increase....

*Faith Communities Today 2010 found 12% of congregations in the US had a **female as senior** or **sole ordained leader**. For **evangelical congregations, it's 9%**.*

ACCESS AND INPUT

READ

"5 Definitive Signs a Church Is Invested in Women," Andrea Ackermann, *Mutuality* blog, November 7, 2017, https://www.cbeinternational.org/resource/article/mutuality-blog-magazine/5-definitive-signs-church-invested-women.

REFLECT

Think of the last three times a woman approached leadership with an idea or concern. What was the response?

Think of the last three times a man approached leadership with an idea or concern. What was the response?

Reflect on the scenarios above: What words were used to respond? What questions were asked? What doubts were expressed? What actions were taken? Were the women believed? Were the men believed? Were their words taken at face value? How much information/supporting data and rationale did the women offer? The men? Did the women have to give more information to be convincing?

When multiple women come forward expressing concerns thatt are similar, are they ever accused of gossip? Are men? What term(s) is used when women share ideas or gather to talk? What term(s) is used when men share ideas or gather to talk? Which group is more likely to be taken seriously? Dismissed? Why?

Thinking back over the last three projects your church implemented, where did these projects originate? How much were women or men engaged in developing/designing them? Who was involved and how were they chosen? Who backed them? Who approved them?

Name ten male experts in the church (on any subject). Name ten female experts in the church (on any subject). Do you notice differences in the lists? Why did these people come to mind most quickly? How does gender play into the way you evaluate them or considered them experts? How should it affect the way the church operates knowing research indicates men have a hard time noticinig women leaders while women have a hard time considering themselves experts and are less likely to assert themselves as experts?

When you have all-church events, who does child care? Who works in the kitchen? Who decorates? Who cleans up? Who works behind the scenes? Who stands up front? Who takes notes? Who makes announcements? Is asked to pray? Offers teaching/the Word? Leads worship? Serve on strategic planning committees, leadership teams or boards? Examine whether women might not be accepting or pursuing leadership roles because they are busy with other work expected of women? Are men willing to fill these roles?

> "The Barna Group found that **female pastors are more likely than male pastors to report** that congregants' **comments on their leadership were "critical," "judging," and "unhelpful."**"

What kind of training do you offer so women/men feel better equipped to volunteer for roles not previously filled by women/men?

Is child care available for all activites or meetings? If not, which meetings or activities do provide child care? Which assumptions underlie when child care is or is not provided? What implications does this have for parents who wish to access activities where child care is not provided? How easy or hard is it for parents to bring their children with them?

Who in your church has access to church financial data and planning, strategic planning documents and spaces, evaluation documents and spaces, decision-making documents and spaces? Do men and women have equal access to this information? Why or why not?

EXPLORE

"Promoting the Partnership of Women in Your Church," Joan Flikkema, *Mutuality* magazine vol. 16, no.3 (2009): 11–15, https://www.cbeinternational.org/resource/article/mutuality-blog-magazine/promoting-partnership-women-your-church.

"Being Egalitarian Isn't Enough: 3 Strategies to Cultivate an Egalitarian Church," Jonathan Schut, *Mutuality* magazine vol. 25, no. 4 (2018): 20–22, https://www.cbeinternational.org/resource/article/mutuality-blog-magazine/being-egalitarian-isnt-enough-3-strategies-cultivate.

In 2017 **women remain less than 25% of the faculty and deans**, and **11% of the presidents** of Association of Theological Schools.[3]

"Men are still more likely than women to be perceived as leaders, study finds," Mattehw Biddle, University at Buffalo News Center, http://www.buffalo.edu/news/news-releases.host.html/content/shared/mgt/news/men-still-more-likely-than-women-perceived-leaders-study-finds.detail.html.

While group size and participants' ages did not affect the gender gap, the study found the length of time participants spent together was an important factor in whether men or women emerged as leaders. The longer a group spent together, the less gender influenced who emerged as the group's leader.

"When What you know is not enough: expertise and gender dynamics in task groups," Millissa C. Thomas-Hunt, Katherine W. Phillips, Personality and Social Psychology Bulletin, December 2004, https://pubmed.ncbi.nlm.nih.gov/15536241/#:~:text=Women%20were%20less%20influential%20when,groups%20with%20a%20male%20expert.

Women were less influential when they possessed expertise, and having expertise decreased how expert others perceived them to be. Conversely, having expertise was relatively positive for men. These differences were reflected in group performance, as groups with a female expert underperformed groups with a male expert. Thus, contrary to common expectations, possessing expertise did not ameliorate the gender effects often seen in workgroups.

Women who had **female congregational leaders in their youth** enjoyed **higher levels of self-esteem as adults.** [4]

---

3. Halee Gray Scott, "Study: Female Pastors Are on the Rise," *Christianity Today*, February 26, 2017, https://www.christianitytoday.com/ct/2017/february-web-only/study-female-pastors-are-on-rise.html, accessed November 12, 2020.
4. Jana Riess, "It's good for girls to have claegywomen, study shows," *Religion News Service*, July 17, 2018, https://religionnews.com/2018/07/17/its-good-for-girls-to-have-clergywomen-study-shows/, accessed October 20,2020

HUMAN RESOURCES

READ

"Single. Female. Pastor," Stephanie Williams, *Mutuality* magazine vol. 21, no. 3 (2014): 12–14, https://www.cbeinternational.org/resources/article/mutuality/single-female-pastor.

REFLECT

Examine your process for hiring: From where do you recruit new staff? Do you recruit from communities that are open to and invitational toward women or are they primarily male communities or institutions (universities, seminaries, denominational pools, etc.)? Are you deliberately recruiting from female-centered or female-promoting communities? Why or why not? Who does the recruiting; men, women, or teams of men and women?

What is your church's family leave policy? Given women are often the primary caretakers of vulnerable family members, a robust family leave policy makes it easeier for women to work at your church. How might your church make caring for family easier to balance when working at your church?

What are your expectations for male candidates versus female candidates with respect to spouse or children? How do you engage candidates without a spouse or children? Is it considered a mark against them? Why or why not? Are there gendered reasons behind your expectations?

What has traditionally been the role of the pastor's spouse in your church? Are expectations different for pastor's spouses who are women versus men?

Look at your job description and hiring questions: How might they be gendered? Are your descriptions based on cultural expectations and norms or biblical expectations and norms? Have you created dompetency based questions so candidates can respond according to their skills? How do salaries compare between male and female employees?

Is the culture in your church prepared to recognize and challenge gendered assumptions? How might it be better prepared?

Notice who is given or who claims credit for projects or decision-making in the church. Are there differences between men and women? Who puts in the most labor? Who gets the credit? Are there examples of times when men took credit for women's ideas?

Ask managers with legal permission to review your staff evaluations from past years. Do you see any patterns when looking at reviews for men versus reviews for women? Were the reviews designed by men and women? Administered by both men and women? Did both men and women have a chance to weigh in?

Which adjectives were used to describe the men on staff? Which adjectives were used to describe the women on staff? What "tone" do those adjectives take on? Note words like aggressive, assertive, confident, gentle, passive, intense, tough, likable, competent, risk-taker, timid, cautious and see if they are applied differently to men or women. Are the characteristics valued differently in women or men? Why or why not? Were there differences in the way raises were given?

Are you aware of the phenomenon of the "glass cliff?" Even when women are hired for higher-level positions, they often lack the support necessary to fully succeed. Additionally, they are often hired to address serious challenges in an organization, and expected to right the course of a vehicle that has been running for years, even decades, in a particular direction. When success does not happen as quickly or dramatically as the organization might hope, the woman is blamed for the failure even though, in many ways, she has been set up to fail. Have you seen it play out in your church?

---

5. Amy Bernstein, "Why Are We So Hard on Female CEOs?", *Harvard Business Review*, May 2015, https://hbr.org/2015/05/why-are-we-so-hard-on-female-ceos, accessed October 12, 2020.

EXPLORE

"The Next Step: Practical Ideas for Egalitarian Churches," Megan Greulich, *Mutuality* magazine vol. 19, no. 2 (2012): 14–15 https://www.cbeinternational.org/resource/article/mutuality-blog-magazine/next-step-practical-ideas-egalitarian-churches.

"Pay gap for women clergy is decreasing, according to new study," David Briggs, *Christian Century*, August 3, 2017, https://www.christiancentury.org/article/pay-gap-women-clergy-decreasing-according-new-study.

> *Married female clergy make around 28 percent less than male clergy. Though the pay gap for women clergy is decreasing (93 cents on the dollar in 2016), the highest paying jobs still are more likely to go to men. Around 21 percent of female clergy are part-time, compared to only 4 percent of male clergy.*
>
> *A 2016 survey of 224 clergywomen in the Evangelical Covenant Church found women "have struggled in finding jobs and are concerned over the underrepresentation of women at all levels of leadership."*

"Why Are We So Hard on Female CEOs?" Amy Bernstein, *Harvard Business Review*, May 2015 issue, https://hbr.org/2015/05/why-are-we-so-hard-on-female-ceos.

> *Studies have shown that women in power exhibit more symptoms of depression, while men in power exhibit fewer. Why? Because, say the researchers, female leaders are seen as abnormal and therefore face resistance. Assertive women are punished for being unfeminine; women who conform to stereotypes are deemed too meek for top jobs.*

"Study: Female Pastors Are on the Rise," Halee Gray Scott, *Christianity Today*, February 26, 2017, https://www.christianitytoday.com/women/2017/february/study-female-pastors-are-on-rise.html.

> *The Barna Group found that female pastors are more likely than male pastors to report that congregants' comments on their leadership were "critical," "judging," and "unhelpful."*

"State of Clergywomen in the United States: A Statistical Update," Eileen Campbell-Reed, 2018, accessed 9/11/2020, https://eileencampbellreed.org/state-of-clergy/.

> " Women whose most influential leader growing up was a woman are equally likely to be employed full-time as men

> *When the Association of Theological Schools in the U.S. and Canada (ATS) began reporting data about gender in 1972–73, women made up just 3 percent of the full-time seminary faculty. In 1998 women were nearly 20 percent of the full-time faculty. In 2017 women remain less than 25 percent of the faculty and deans, and 11 percent of the presidents of ATS schools.*
>
> *In 1973 women were less than 5 in every 100 Master of Divinity (MDiv) students, and only 10 percent of overall seminary enrollments. In the next 25 years, the numbers shot up. By 1998, 30 of every 100 MDiv students in the U.S. and Canada, and 33 out of 100 students in all seminary programs (masters and doctoral level) were women.*
>
> *The story of the past twenty years, however, appears to be one of stagnation. In 2017 women are actually a smaller number and a lower percentage of MDiv Students in all ATS schools than they were in 1998.*

CULTURE OF WORK AND FAMILY

READ

"4 Jobs Women Are Expected to Do without Pay, and How to Balance the Labor Scale," Rachel Asproth, *Mutuality* magazine vol. 26, no 1 (2019): 16–21, https://www.cbeinternational.org/resource/article/mutuality-blog-magazine/4-jobs-women-are-expected-do-without-pay-and-how-balance.

REFLECT

What is your church teaching about biblical motherhood? Biblical fatherhood? Are there differences in what makes a good mom versus what makes a good dad? What does your church teach about working outside the home? Working inside the home? Are teachings/ sermons designed assuming all women or all men do or do not work outside the home? What is the impact of this assumption?

Is there a mom's/ dad's ministry? Is there a men's and women's Bible study or prayer group? Are the meetings/ activities scheduled at convenient times for those who work outside the home as for those who don't? Is there a place for stay-at-home dads to receive support?

What are other examples in your church of women or men who are engaged in vocations not fitting traditional gender roles?

How is the church offering support for non-traditional work to which men or women are called? Have you asked them if they feel supported or what they might need to feel supported?

How is your church ministering to singles? What teaching are they receiving about their identity as singles? Is the teaching different depending on gender? If it is, does Scripture support the different teachings offered?

EXPLORE

"Our Dual-Career Family: Benefits and Challenges," Dwayne J. Howell and Susan Howell, 2006, https://www.cbeinternational.org/resource/article/our-dual-career-family.

"Stay at Home Dad," MaryAnn Nguyen-Kwok, *Mutuality* blog, July 12, 2011, https://www.cbeinternational.org/resource/article/mutuality-blog-magazine/stay-home-dads

"Freeing Women to Pursue Diverse Callings," Alexis Waggoner, *Mutuality* blog, June 30, 2016, https://www.cbeinternational.org/resource/article/mutuality-blog-magazine/freeing-women-pursue-diverse-callings.

RESOURCES AND TEACHING MATERIALS

READ

"The Subtle Hazing of Women in Ministry," Jill Richardson, *Mutuality* blog, November 6, 2019, https://www.cbeinternational.org/resource/article/mutuality-blog-magazine/subtle-hazing-women-ministry.

REFLECT

For any teaching materials, resources, or curricula you offer including those for parenting, family, children and youth, women's or men's Bible studies, singles ministry, or pre-marital counseling, consider:

Which gender assumptions are built into the teachings or curriculum? How are the men/boys portrayed? How are the women/girls portrayed? Which roles are they called into? Encouraged to pursue?

When illustrations or anecdotes are offered, how do men/boys appear/sound? How do women/girls appear/sound? What actions do men/boys or women/girls take in the examples given? Are there patterns in the way men/boys or women/girls are portrayed?

Which biblical characters are emphasized in your teachings or curricula? What roles do they play in the illustrations offered? Are they the helper? Rescuer? Protector? Servant? Leader? Are they strong? Weak? Dependent? Independent? Why?

When young men in your church grow up, what jobs/roles do they tend to pursue? When young women in your church grow up, what jobs/roles do they tend to pursue? Are there any patterns? What might those patterns reveal?

Are teachers and leaders trained to be aware of these things and to check their biases? Is this an intentional emphasis of the church?

EXPLORE

"Biological Determinism and the 'Oughtness' of Manhood," Aaron Sathyanesan, *Mutuality* blog, August 12, 2015, https://www.cbeinternational.org/resource/article/mutuality-blog-magazine/biological-determinism-and-oughtness-manhood.

"Puzzling Reflections," Amy R. Buckley, *Mutuality* magazine vol 22, no. 3, (2015): 7–9, https://www.cbeinternational.org/resource/article/mutuality-blog-magazine/puzzling-reflections.

"Girl Brain? Boy Brain?: A Neuroscientist Examines The Evidence," Aaron Sathyanesan, *Mutuality* blog, December 21, 2015, https://www.cbeinternational.org/resource/article/mutuality-blog-magazine/girl-brain-boy-brain-neuroscientist-examines-evidence.

LITURGY AND CHURCH TRADITIONS

READ

"What Language Shall We Use?" Mimi Haddad, *Priscilla Papers vol.* 17, no. 1 (2003): 3-7, https://www.cbeinternational.org/resource/article/priscilla-papers-academic-journal/what-language-shall-we-use-look-inclusive.

REFLECT

Consider the way art, drama, readings, images, and music are chosen for services and events: Who chose/chooses them? Were/are under-represented groups asked for input in choosing?

Are there both male and female images and characters represented in liturgy/tradition/art in your church?

In those formats, how are the men portrayed? How are the women portrayed? What actions are they taking when depicted in stories or songs or pictures? Are they the helper? Rescuer? Protector? Servant? Leader? Are they strong? Weak? Dependent? Independent? Why?

Which biblical characters feature most prominently in your church's art, drama, readings, images, and music? Are both men and women represented? Why or why not?

What roles do men play in various elements of liturgy/tradition? What roles do women play? Why?

> "In Wurttemberg's Protestant churches, baroque female angels appeared in important and powerful roles. For example, female figures support the pulpits in the churches of Altheim and Langenaue. In a 1734 painting in the church of Hurben, the judges who decided between heaven and hell in the Last Judgement were women angels."

EXPLORE

"Gender Language in Worship," Jeffrey D. Miller, Conference Presentation, July 2013, https://www.cbeinternational.org/resources/recording-audio/gender-language-worship.

"Women and Liturgical Reform: The Case of St. Margaret of Scotland," Bridget Nichols, *Priscilla Papers* vol. 22, no. 1 (2008): 23-28, https://www.cbeinternational.org/resource/article/priscilla-papers-academic-journal/women-and-liturgical-reform.

"The Representation of Women in Religious Art and Imagery: Discontinuities in "Female virtues", Stefanie Schäfer-Bossert, *Gender in Transition: Discourse and Practice in German-Speaking Europe 1750–1830*, https://www.press.umich.edu/pdf/9780472099436-ch6.pdf

Women's images were not always so poorly represented in church art. During Sattelzeit ("saddle time"), a period between 1750 and 1870, female images of the divine were targeted for change or removal. Not only female images, but any image which "did not directly conform to prescribed social reality" was eliminated. Prior to this time, there was greater representation of female images which portrayed spiritual strength. For example, often the Holy Spirit appeared as a woman, "the mother of the virtues, the daughters whom she bore and in whom she was present. The terms Charity, Holy Spirit, and Mother were often used interchangeably."

"Men's as well as women's souls were considered to be female, and every human soul was preordained to be the bride of Christ. Death sometimes was represented as the female soul leaving a male body." In popular illustrated Bibles, (17th century) the angels in Jacob's vision of the ladder are female. "In Wurttemberg's Protestant churches, baroque female angels appeared in important and powerful roles. For example, female figures support the pulpits in the churches of Altheim and Langenaue. In a 1734 painting in the church of Hurben, the judges who decided between heaven and hell in the Last Judgement were women angels."

> "During Sattelzeit ("saddle time"), a period between 1750 and 1870, female images of the divine were targeted for change or removal."

Nurturing Women's Equality - A Church Evaluation Tool

MINISTRY ACTIVITIES

READ

"Will Boys Be Boys and Girls Be Girls?," David Csinos, *Priscilla Papers* vol. 31, no. 4 (2017), https://www.cbeinternational.org/resources/article/other/modesty.

REFLECT

How are events designed for men? For women? Boys? Girls? Who designs them? Do the activities reflect gender bias? What is the impact of these decisions?

Are there opportunities for men/boys to engage in activities which promote emotional vulnerability and connection?

Are there opportunities for women/girls to engage in activities that promote physical activity or competition?

Are there dress codes for the youth group? Do differences exist in how they're they applied to girls or boys? Why? Are girls expected to protect boys from temptation? Do youth leaders talk about double-standards for boys and girls or do they parrot popular teachings that put the responsibility on girls to "keep their brothers from stumbling," etc.

What are you teaching boys/men and girls/women about consent in and outside of marriage?

What resources do you use for pre-marriage counseling? Are the teachings or reflections based on gender stereotypes? What kinds of expectations for gender roles are projected?

What are you teaching boys/men and girls/women about decision-making between spouses?

Do teachings reflect gendered identities, one for males and another for females?

If a spouse comes to a leader and reports s/he's been abused, what is your church policy for how to handle it? Are staff and volunteers trained to engage these issues? Has anyone in leadership encouraged women/ men to stay in abusive relationships for any reason? What resources are available for women/ men in these circumstances?

EXPLORE

"Defending My Daughters against Rape Culture," Eugene Hung, *Mutuality* magazine vol. 24, no. 1 (2017): 14-15, https://www.cbeinternational.org/resource/article/mutuality-blog-magazine/defending-my-daughters-against-rape-culture.

"It's Time for a Sexual Ethic Jesus Might Have Actually Preached," Lyndsey Medford, *Mutuality* magazine vol. 26, no. 2 (2019): 24-26, https://www.cbeinternational.org/resource/article/mutuality-blog-magazine/its-time-sexual-ethic-jesus-might-have-actually-preached.

"Egalitarianism Is for Men, Too," J. W. Wartick, *Mutuality* blog, December 9, 2015, https://www.cbeinternational.org/resource/article/mutuality-blog-magazine/egalitarianism-men-too.

"Modesty: A Word for Boys and Girls," Marissa Cwik, https://www.cbeinternational.org/resource/article/modesty.

"10 Myths About Domestic Abuse You Didn't Know You Believed: Part 1," Natalie Collins, *Mutuality* blog, October 25, 2015, https://www.cbeinternational.org/resource/article/mutuality-blog-magazine/10-myths-about-domestic-abuse-you-didnt-know-you-believed.

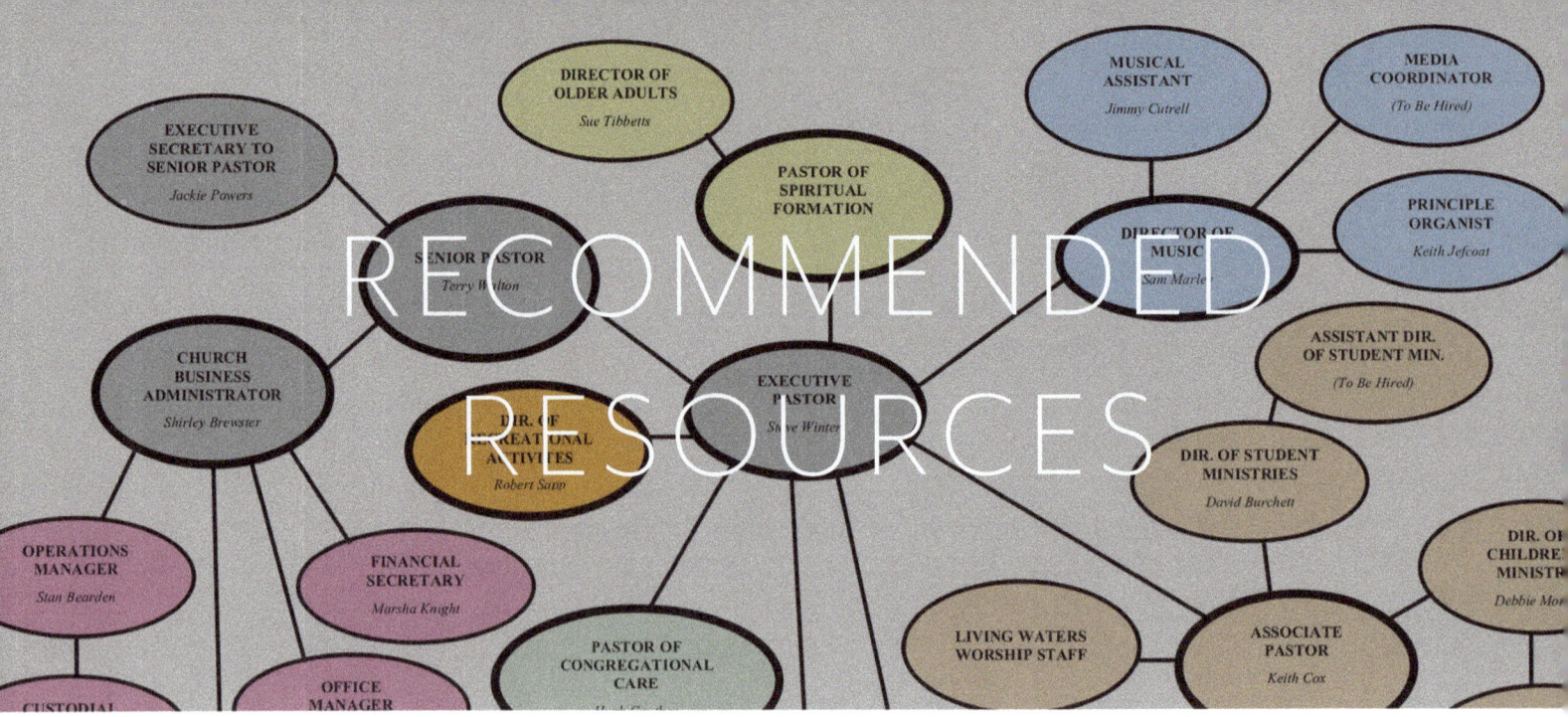

RECOMMENDED RESOURCES

ARTICLES

"Is God Male? A Five-Part Series, (Part 1)" Mimi Haddad, *Mutuality* blog, April 24, 2012, https://www.cbeinternational.org/resource/article/mutuality-blog-magazine/god-male-part-1-worship-male-god.

"Womanism, Intersectionality, and Biblical Justice," Mitzi J. Smith, *Mutuality* magazine vol. 23, no. 2, https://www.cbeinternational.org/resource/article/mutuality-blog-magazine/womanism-intersectionality-and-biblical-justice.

"There's Something in the Water: How Second-Generation Gender Bias Makes it Difficult for Women Leaders to Thrive," Stephani Dyrness Lobdell, *Christianity Today*, https://www.christianitytoday.com/women-leaders/2018/january/theres-something-in-water.html.

"The Urgency of Intersectionality," Kimberé Williams Crenshaw, https://www.ted.com/talks/kimberle_crenshaw_the_urgency_of_intersectionality?language=en.

Harvard's implicit bias tests, particularly the Gender-Career IAT. https://implicit.harvard.edu/implicit/takeatest.html.

"After Willow Creek: How Can Churches Make Women Feel Safe Again?" Kelly Ladd Bishop, *Mutuality* blog, https://www.cbeinternational.org/resource/article/mutuality-blog-magazine/after-willow-creek-how-can-churches-make-women-feel-safe.

"Speaking of Justice: 10 Terms Christian Gender Justice Advocates Should Know," Rachel Asproth, *Mutuality* magazine vol. 23, no. 2, https://www.cbeinternational.org/resource/article/mutuality-blog-magazine/speaking-justice-10-terms-christian-gender-justice.

"15 Books on Domestic Violence for Pastors, Believers, and Survivors," CBE International, *Mutuality* blog, October 8, 2018, https://www.cbeinternational.org/resource/article/mutuality-blog-magazine/15-books-domestic-violence-pastors-believers-and-survivors.

"The Invisible Knapsack of Male Privilege in the Church," Rachel Asproth, *Mutuality* blog, https://www.cbeinternational.org/resource/article/mutuality-blog-magazine/invisible-knapsack-male-privilege-church.

BOOKS

Discovering Biblical Equality: Biblical, Theological, Cultural, and Practical Perspectives edited by Ronald W. Pierce, Cynthia Long Westfall, and Christa L. McKirland

As Christ Submits to the Church: A Biblical Understanding of Leadership and Mutual Submission by Alan G. Padgett

Making Room for Leadership: Power, Space and Influence by MaryKate Morse

Is Women's Equality a Biblical Ideal? A Five-Part Series by Mimi Haddad (book and video)

The Moment of Lift: How Empowering Women Changes the World by Melinda Gates

Made to Lead: Empowering Women for Ministry by Nicole Massie Martin

Building a Church Full of Leaders by Jeanne Porter King

Global Voices on Biblical Equality: Women and Men Ministering Together in the Church edited by Aída Besançon Spencer, William Spencer, and Mimi Haddad

Rediscovering Scripture's Vision for Women: Fresh Perspectives on Disputed Texts **by Lucy Peppiatt**

Together in Ministry: Women and Men in Flourishing Partnerships by Rob Dixon

Created to Thrive: Cultivating Abuse-Free Faith Communities, edited by Elizabeth Beyer

AUDIO/VIDEO

"Women's Leadership at the Highest Level: Plateaus and Pitfalls," Shirley Mullen, https://www.cbeinternational.org/resource/audio/womens-leadership-highest-level-plateaus-and-pitfalls.

"Take Every Thought Captive to Christ: Ideas Have Consequences," Mimi Haddad, https://www.cbeinternational.org/resource/video/take-every-thought-captive-christ-ideas-have-consequences.

"Advancing Women Into Leadership: Why This Matters and How to Reach that Goal," Karen Longman, https://www.cbeinternational.org/resource/audio/advancing-women-leadership-why-matters-and-how-reach-goal.

"Creating a Paradigm Shift in Denominational Practices," Frank Stevenson, https://www.cbeinternational.org/resource/audio/creating-paradigm-shift-denominational-practices.

"Women's Ordination as Pastors: A Middle Eastern Perspective," Anne Zaki, https://www.cbeinternational.org/resource/video/womens-ordination-pastors-middle-eastern-perspective.

"Misogyny in the Church," Eugene Cho, https://www.cbeinternational.org/resource/video/misogyny-church.

"Pastor's Panel," Eugene Cho, Anne Zaki, Adelita Garza, https://www.cbeinternational.org/resource/audio/pastors-panel.

www.ingramcontent.com/pod-product-compliance
Lightning Source LLC
Chambersburg PA
CBHW081509040426
42446CB00017B/3445